ANGUISH: A POETESS IN LOVE OR A WARRIOR IN DISGUISE?

SCARLETT HOPE

Copyright © Scarlett Hope
All Rights Reserved.

Life's journey should always be unpredictable where you find new souls and experience each and every emotion with passion and honesty. Unless you suffer, life's longings lie incomplete and perplexed.

I've acknowledged my phases, the emotions I've gone through, and even the highly unbearable ones are resting close to my fragile heart. Sometimes, it's the mirror you need, to look beyond your reach, to realize where you really belong.

This book is my reality and my daydream dedicated to all the people I met, loved, lost, and yearned to be a part of this misery.

Thank you for all the lessons, for loving and showing kindness, for making me aware of my flaws, and for breaking my heart into a million pieces that I can never fix, not even in my dreams.

Contents

Contents

Preface

There is no escape if you don't exhale, the more you keep it to your heart, the more you suffer. For years, I was taught to remain silent, to never utter a word that contradicts the norms, and that made me weak, enclosed in the four walls of a room can be terribly horrifying. And so I chose strength for some years and then I fell back into the maze yet again. My never-ending fears drowned all my hopes and the urge to swim and reach the shore.

Poetry is a way to evade the silence, tolerate the pain of loneliness, and forget the scars of my outrageous expressions. I am a failure when I speak, my words are all tangled with the chaos in my heart and the fear to lose, so they hold no worth to the listener. But I've got the power in my hands when I write because that's where I control my mind, filter my thoughts, and understand what's truly inside...

1. Beginning

"*Every new chapter that your fate has created,, begins with losses and pain...*
Invisible to those ocean blue eyes, it grows within your soul and erupts with with time, a journey through oblivion making its way to your consciousness!"

HOPE- Chapter 1

Hope

If you've grown up a little different,

like a traumatic journey that you wanted to change...

So you begged to God crying,

sometimes you prayed silently so that no one knows,

in doubt, if they don't let you grow better than you were those days!

Weird sort of fear, you never felt before...

Then you learnt to "hope",

to have faith and to believe that it never stays forever!

But it kept on happening again and again making you so weird, anxious, insecure...

You left yourself somewhere, too far!

You stopped believing what you believed in,

Had this baseless hate for yourself,

like it's almost done for you...

But then suddenly "hope" walks in!

The moment you felt like ending it,

someone came, to hold you...

Made you feel,

what you never thought you could

You did everything...

that you never dreamt of!

It felt beautiful...

So much warmth,

You named it Love!

It stayed as it promised to...

Though you were the same!

Stuck on dreaming, clumsy, anxious, inexpressive and weird...

You were sick, not like those physical pain, it was all in your head,

dumped after years of trauma!

But somehow you would never let go of your "hope"...

You believed, his love might heal!

Then you realised that wasn't love,

It faded away, leaving you all lost...

He wasn't the one who understood who you were...

He never loved you, but your face!

It was an infatuation,

believed to be your first love!

He never cared, he never felt, not that he tried!

But he kept saying every day, that he loves you...

So it broke you even more!

Like everyone you met, came into your life...

somehow pushed you to fall and turned you dark and lonely.

They've changed maybe,

but you stayed there confused and shattered!

That confidence you gathered,

the guts you had, those dreams you aimed for...

started leaving you one by one!

You shouted, pleaded with them to stay...

Maybe they were deaf,

you consoled 'cause it was too hard to end yourself,

giving pain to others that you felt lying alone every day!

It was "hope", that you never felt...

Though everyone was around you,

but your heart went cold,

you were living 'cause you had to!

No one believed, no one cared as days passed by...

So you wrote, believing they will miss what they've lost while ignoring,

you were trying to fight for all your life!

2. Chaos

What if

What if you are grasped by something irrelevant and completely abstract?

What if you struggle every day and get back to where you started?

What if you discover, that void in your heart is irreplaceable?

What if you are crying like you've lost someone close to you, but actually, the reality is lying somewhere in the universe, too far away from your heart?

What if you know what you want but can't even make the first move to get close to it?

What if you are buried with something known yet unknown, that bursts and comes out to be like, you are in a vicious circle when you cry being unconscious?

What if you are exactly lying in your possibilities where you thought you could be someday?

What if, that "every morning will be a new seed of hope, being nourished to let it grow, into a beautiful tree of betterment" turns out to be the end, masked by your fake optimism?

Perception till death

Of a moon, not so bright...

Crumbling stars,

Infinite faults, there in the sky

For humans', wanting birds to dive and whales to fly!

Imperfections being unconventional,

Questioning self-doubts

Believing perspectives all around!

Society spilling buckets of truth,

And you're a liar, living and eating lies...

Only if hypocrisy had heights,

There'll be people walking through the skies!

You and me, we all are ants...

Smashed by paws, we've no life!

We're evolved middle-aged goons,

Actors behind cells, knocking out fools.

Pretending love,

Breaking hearts...

And moving on!

Murmuring, "Yes, this is life!"

Emptied cans, no coins

Confused and shattered vines...

A void is so deep!

But this race, there's no time to breathe...

Sometimes, waves turn into storms...

Glitching emotions, no stability, destructing own norms!

A queue so long, waiting...

For you to crumble,

neighbours, praying stars!

Of a world, where death is precise...

Your prayers are so ruined.

Don't you worry, the corpses you wished to be living...

Spectating you up from the sky!

Cursing, so you die.

Falling

There have been days,

I stared at the ceiling

thinking, how I am falling!

Same old diaries,

Inked feelings

Smudged by drops

When I was too numb to speak...

Though I was overwhelmed,

Awkward, little stammering voice,

Repressed thoughts...

Stayed in me!

I would want to say a lot

Then, I would be all tired

Scared, anxious, and worried,

That I've to fight it all

alone at the moment!

There were days,

I would feel so much hate

'cause I couldn't fit their ways!

The world is too defined,

to live in...

There are too many opinions

Enough to cut your wings,

'cause no one likes to see you fly!

And sleep dreaming,

Soulful nights...

If eyes could speak

If eyes could speak,

I would have shown you,

How it feels...

How silence screams,

How this inevitable pain

breaks your heart,

Grabs your feet

and pulls you down

in the deep,

Too dark to see!

A never-ending void...

If eyes could speak,

I would have shown you

what my lips couldn't speak!

Nomad

Just another day off in awe,

how looking at the clouds, feels like...

So high on life,

tripping again and again!

It no longer feels heavy,

and more stuck with

how this chaotic world constantly pulling me hard,

yet losing its grip...

I am the one lost,

you all are running legacy...

I am the one abandoned,

living all dizzy,

where time personified storms,

vibing my enthusiasm,

all numb when I am tired, raining when I cry,

getting me over these false memories and making me more poetic, painting a world where I would live while dying...

Just another day,

someone else being mobbed by the silence I was living with,

hunting happiness,

seen lying beside my grave!

Yet, I am the one,

looking at the clouds,

raining in grief...

how I left the world in pain...

Out of the ordinary

Brewing that chaos in myself

seeing her dancing sorrows

through my eyes...

Raining dense off-road

with no signs of life,

just that melody in my head

and her heavy eyes

fused in me

and I could see

it's my soul growling,

fumed in anger,

questioning...

if I still need to exist

or she could rip off my chest

and free her pain

into the rain

dancing up in the sky...

It's just me,

lying so beautifully penning that melody

through my tears...

So peaceful as I go leaving myself happier,

I've ever been!

Humming

Same old stories that I told you everyday...

Those sunflowers in my dream yard,

understands when I stare at 'em,

And when I tend to yell...

My wings start flapping,

The blowing wind turns into a storm,

Wanting to detach my feet from the ground!

So stubborn, uprooted trees all around...

Branches swinging back and forth!

Like it has planned to destroy all my wounds...

Those scratches, bruised chest and broken hands,

Half burnt croissants, sometimes shared by ants!

When you have nothing to feel!

Don't have enough to feed!

But your struggling mind still working

like those cabled TVs without pictures and smiles...

Listening to those flashing memories from the sky.

I left my sunflowers teary eyed...

I tried hugging the storm

Said my pain isn't worth bleeding on

their broken hearts,

He frowned!

I said,

"Little fragile, still trying to live!"

But how weird is it,

When someone feels your failing dreams...

Feel you, in your long lost soul

Trapped in a maze,

where your heartbeats skipped

Too many void, to keep!

But, I felt loved...

My heart is already healed!

I tapped down...

Looked at the sky,

Then I saw

Clouds started raining,

The raindrops fell on the petals

Conveying there's beauty in your

heartaches and your pain!

It was freezing cold that day...

Drenched clothes, and my confused state...

Dried lips, frozen feet...

I fainted under my wondering head,

When I heard

Creepy little creatures were passing

through the shade!

Oh...

An unbearable night,

Blinking stars singing lullaby

I frowned,

reflected rays warming up the frozen grounds...

I woke up, rubbing my dizzy eyes;

The windows were wide open...

And beams of light swallowing darkness,

I saw a beautiful sunrise!

Pearls dripping from the petals;

Shining, bright yellow sunflowers

owning my infectious smile...

As I shower!

Notebooks and torn pages,

Scattered all around...

A penned note on the ground,

Reminding the befitting night

I spent in my godown!

The way I am

Why do I hate the way I am?

Why I can't be the way I was?

Negotiating, what that means...

What everything means and why me?

Is everything real or just a dream...

Would fade away tomorrow,

my existence, my memories!

Then, you would hardly believe,

A pain in your arms, you would want to forget...

A beginning you never saw and an end you are destined to write!

Why do I hope, knowing I can't see the stars in you?

Lies

They see you shine,

But never understood why...

Years of trauma,

Still they see you smile...

Like you scream all alone at night

And they'll be listening why,

Some pretend to stay

You chose them,

Then you push the one

Who wanted to be there...

That's insane!

As you wake up all night,

Incomplete...

You see the moon cry

Like it feels your pain,

But, can't stay by your side

There's the burning sun outside.

Just another day;

You see yourself lie...

That you're sparkling,

Shining so bright

Laughing, teary eyed!

Drifting

Faling stars,

my dreams floating so high...

some preoccupied failures grabbed my soul

and chained my life!

The scars, those uprooted bushes

and my screaming soul saw how I was flying high,

My dreams by my side...

A lost child wrapping stars,

and my sleepy eyes!

Strangers

A smile so warm,

such laughing weird faces, to die for...

gone somewhere,

while pretending to be someone,

so like that "stranger",

I would hardly ever talk to...

and loving my real self!

Musing, what went wrong in me for so long,

that I am annoyed with that smile when it tends to interrupt...

while faking my laughter with that "stranger",

I am dying for...

To the torn pages of my diary

I promise,

I shall forever be with you...

And you will keep me safe and untouched

even if I free my pain in the end,

burying my bones down in the deep...

so I scatter into pieces fleeing up in the sky,

falling down when it rains,

deeper into the eroded soil while waving back in the ocean!

I shall always come back,

remember you have my remains...

Inked pain of secrets,

I left in your heart...

so you scream throwing me away,

my remains...

Showing secrets in the streets,

just like those fall leaves!

I shall be smiling,

that you made me an infinite melody...

My remains

Sometimes there's no you and me,

But an undesirable void in my heart

and an aching silence

increasing my heartbeat for no reason...

It's simply the fear to lose something,

I would obviously not,

but that, I can't help

'cause sometimes,

the most obvious things that you love the most...

relentlessly breaks your trust

and treats you like,

You're not human

but a man's creation to be controlled!

And they...

They do nothing,

But watch your melancholy

from the spectator's seat!

Apprehension

Shattered dreams,

Still...

Never stopped thinking!

A failing life,

Breathing sighs...

Still living!

Wondering, all I couldn't have

Teary-eyed,

Still smiling...

I prayed each night,

Still,

I've seen folks, leaving!

Making me worthless,

Not too many reasons,

I could live for

I am still praying,

In hope...

I would have someone

Flowering my grave...

Remembering,

How I never stopped loving;

Till death!

Reverie

She is dreaming every now and then,

Escaping home ambled along the road to death...

They say,

what is life without fear and regrets?

Have faith;

But until when...

Wandering around the visions of utopia;

Embedded dawn of soreness!

Disbelieving her every step,

Pretentious to everyone she met,

They say,

but what is life without aloneness?

Alienating people,

Signs of her anthropophobia...

Closed casements accompanied her sheer darkness;

Entwined in her flickering daydreams,

She is scared of her reflections,

Penned imperfections...

Gleaming on her secret reams!

Once, she believed,

would bear off her wilderness...

They were drowning,

The erosions of her mind...

She is, Hope

Treading water to keep afloat...

Icebergs made of her trauma feel so inclined;

Losing steadiness in the shallows,

Deeper into oblivion,

she is helplessly screaming!

3. When he came through

"Love is conditioned to be painful and lonely, yet a desire, inescapable till you perish, leaving your remains in memories, to be nurtured by those who longed to have you, and to those who failed to cherish your existence!"

Dark

For you to be with me, I've nothing to give.

I am an entire ocean where the livings die,

too shallow they can't even breathe!

I am living in my own grave,

my eyes are red...

It is raining outside so heavy,

that the water is gliding,

making it too patchy to let anyone in!

I've nothing to give...

Scribbled stories, my penned echoes

grabbing you down in the deep,

too dark to see...

Where you've got an open yard to dream,

where time stops...

the sun sets too long,

where you wait till your pen stops

for the wind to fool you to the maze

you never craved for!

You see me wherever you go...

it's all a lie!

Just close your eyes and run,

I've seen them too.

They drive you insane,

remember I told you, the time we were locked!

I didn't know, I would turn so dark...

entangled illusions,

a never-ending maze dragging you down, so deep!

Screaming silence,

regretting that you've fallen,

yet planning ways so you heat the demons inside me...

chasing!

Pale-faced, too fragile...

you can't even touch!

A yard blew by feelings,

pages grabbing your hands,

too many voids,

you would never know,

where to start from!

Thoughts dealing storms every day...

too tired to even utter a word.

Taming you, so you understand,

upsetting when you don't...

There's nothing left to hold on love...

I've no cents,

you'll be walking through it all your life!

But I loved you, more than my life

yet I've nothing to give...

So, I want you to leave.

My first rain

It was raining so far...

I was crying so hard,

A quiet and most painful night I've ever seen,

My heart was aching within...

To be honest, that day I couldn't stop crying.

I was trying to hold back my tears;

in fear, so that no one could hear!

But I say, I'm thankful to you "rain",

your fellas, the "wind" and the "train".

My phone was ringing,

I ignored it, gone sleeping.

Constantly praying, the night to pass...

So I could ask, "was it prompt to say it all?"

I heard someone, tapping on the ground,

I opened my eyes and found...

The ocean in the sky,

clouds turning into species,

"Oh so creepy...!"

I frowned,

I saw the sharks around...

It was my first dive into the blue.

But wait, was it all an illusion?

'cause everything started to fade,

the clouds burst and I lost it all!

For a moment, it was a string of happiness gathered

from my span of life so far;

Fortunately, it couldn't last!

I woke up hearing voices out loud,

Of cursed angles begging for hunger in the crowd;

The sunshine covering the marks of their sins...

I patted my head, remembered the fins;

And then I saw the man, who would be my past soon!

My eyes were still red, with drops of blood from the sides;

Burning to the core, so does my heart...

It was not the pain to lose anymore,

But of rage to go and to find me even more.

This too shall pass;

And thank you to the "rain" alas!

You and I

I thought you would stay a little more,

I thought you would be silly today...

I was upset,

But then I realised that's all you have for me,

You just walked away!

Though it was the same feeling,

that we're so close...

But now it's a bit different I guess!

You fell so bad, though I was all lost that day...

I wish I could say, I am falling deeper each day!

It's so dark here and I am scared to lose it all...

"Please come back, save me if you can!"

my soul was shouting and you couldn't listen,

you just walked away!

I waited, thought you would call me up

like I do every day...

And you didn't as expected!

But then I let it go, 'cause I want you to stay!

In the end, just make sure, you don't walk away...

I won't be funny some days,

Would be quiet and weird...

I can't control that but it's up to you,

How you would react!

Like I was there, laughing to make sure you smile;

You feel comfort even though I was broken inside...

Somehow I expect you to do the same,

I've no one around at the end of the day!

You can't bear what I am feeling,

But I need you to understand this...

It's too hard to heal,

Just make sure you don't add much

'cause it's a whole lot of trash to speak!

I am not sure if you know,

But you've got this confidence no matter what you do!

You love yourself way more than I do...

But then you've to divide that,

Remember you said, you love me too!

Of course, I would be wrong some days,

Just to let you know, I apologise to make it all okay!

And there you go,

You don't even take my point when I say!

You get all defensive, screw everything on my way...

And you're all same the other day!

I know I can't express,

I would keep everything to myself and mourn instead...

I am quite not predictable as you think dear...

You only know the things I chose to tell you,

But there's an ocean full of secrets that I would know and certainly not you!

Honestly, I don't want to say,

'cause I don't trust you anymore!

I know halfway through,

You would put the blame on me...

'cause you don't know how heavy it feels

to carry those feelings as you've never been there

unlike me!

I can tell you one thing for sure,

If I feel like this one more time from now...

I am choosing my memories, not you!

I won't come back again,

And I would make sure...

When I'll die in my grave,

Your shadow to not even pass my frame!

Ungrateful

Those unforgettable nights, I've spent all alone...

Those scars you never knew,

are growing even more...

I hope you find peace knowing,

how vulnerable my emotions were!

Though you've never been there...

They taught you to never leave,

But never enlightened you how!

So, you left me leaning incomplete,

knowing I would crawl each day and you'll be playing around...

You knew how fragile I am and you let me fall;

Too soon, my broken legs, not knowing how to stand up!

But you weren't there somehow.

So, dare to be that man, "playing" better songs;

And try to stand where you belong,

I may not be perfect...

Like you are,

But I don't pretend to be one, then and now...

I'm still diving into my sorrows;

Too deep, that you may drown...

I hope you find peace knowing I still have my crown!

Gray (Ballade)

A whole day without you means, infinite nightmares...

means, anxiety, freckles on my face,

little anger turning an ocean of my tears;

Nights so cold, freezing hands still out with the phone,

waiting so it rings like that 12 a.m to 4 a.m talks...

Felt so short, like it envies happy souls!

Those broken long stories...

like remembering our lost childhood for a while;

Like those phone conversations to tempting kisses we shared...

All my first time!

It's never the same, whether it's hate or love...

One with a smile, the other one cries,

Sometimes, it's just the bad times...

Often, everything seems so unfair

Like, I shall wait, thinking all day, stuck on dreaming, day and night!

You'll be busy, tired, and sleepy,

Playing games with my mind...

For you,

Love is, my lips on yours...

Conveying, I am everything, you were looking for!

For me,

Love is, the one thing I never got...

Feelings so strong, and a broken heart,

Crawling so you hold for once,

After a day, like decades of pain...

Your voice for once, I was craving for!

All you have is, "everything you wanted"

And, all I have is, "my numb thoughts"

Loud enough,

my veins to burst...

Bloody tears and my drenched clothes;

A whole day without you means, infinite scars...

means broken limbs and a ghost heart!

A wasted memory

Would you remember me tonight?

Like every winter night,

freezing your heart with my warm hands

and my drenched collection of your memories...

Would you remember me tonight?

Like my sobbing eyes on your empty notes,

making more of something, I know, would never exist!

Would you remember me tonight?

Like our cold conversations every time...

Like our last goodbyes,

fleeing back to our godowns,

like we've never met before,

but more of those strangers we've had stories in our hearts about,

every passing day!

Would you remember me tonight?

Like you had my eyes on that raining lane...

tearing my own skin,

to fix your broken yearning!

A red rose, that you never carried for,

leaving it somewhere, unwanted!

Would you remember me tonight?

Like my tears and your revengeful sight,

just an autumn leaf, dying to live,

unlike those fallen leaves drying on the streets!

When I fell for you

I smell your love when you aren't there!

your sweatshirt, a memory of that night...

we were all drenched, holding each other's hands...

That raining night!

Your eyes are on mine and my little awkward smile...

Being so weird but myself,

You're that comfort

I wore it every day!

From sleepless nights...

Sharing our life together,

I still never felt enough

Like I would stay all-day

All my life

Craving you, only you...

Your voice felt like a melody,

I would hug to sleep.

Your absence is my burning chaos,

I would make more of you in my mind

On my little notes, I kept writing for you!

Remembering all my first times...

You're that pain,

I would bear it all my life!

Smiling, that you're here

Though you broke my heart

And that ain't fair!

Exhortation

Feels so weak,

When I see your glazed eyes!

Someone screams, saying...

"Who are you?"

Who am I?

Without you...

I wonder!

The confused state of guilt,

You poured into me

'cause I asked you to care!

Asked you to be there,

When I was dumped all alone

trembling in fear...

Delusional,

Hearing footsteps,

Guns in their hands

Banging the door...

So close to the end

I wonder!

Bleeding eyes...

'cause I can't close them

Can't sleep,

They get stronger

When I am not myself

But it never felt alright

Messy hair, dry lips,

Holding my knees, so tight

An illusion in filth,

Or my fear?

Sweating anxiety...

Bruised hands,

While screaming confused;

Scratching my skin

Oh, such a frightful sight!

Constantly overhearing voices

Not meant for me...

A secret,

Would you ever believe it?

I wonder!

Exhausted,

No more consolation

I started hating myself!

But then, I had to hold on

I had responsibilities ahead!

Couldn't bear the pain...

But I had no way to say,

"Can't live, I am dying instead!"

So I calmed my head,

Blaming my fate...

Gently closing my chaos

my sobbing eyes,

in my pillows;

I fell asleep,

Dreaming about my favourite shows

That I made for years,

"My life in a nutshell!"

Everything I wished for!

Sometimes I think...

Will, it ever be enough,

to be free?

Will I ever be enough,

to be the one you wished to love,

to feel what you would for someone else?

I wonder!

While running back and forth

dreaming my days,

that I couldn't find anywhere else...

Choking into reality

yet finding new ways,

to touch your thoughts...

To see if I could find the soul

that I was searching for!

A sweet delight in your endless nights?

Or a listless weaver in distress,

sewing her melancholy...

That you would comprehend in denial,

Off the shore singing Lullaby?

I wonder!

Before leaving my soul,

into the grave of hope,

I want you to know,

There's an old case,

I kept it for you in the attic...

My emotions buried inside a penned note,

lying barely on the ground,

dusted leaves, covered with webs all around...

Would you ever search for?

or would you let it decay,

until you erase my memories,

accompanied by moulds?

I wonder!

Passion

I want to love you like,

You're the broken string I'm fixing,

Holding your heart delicately,

Though I'm drifting,

knowing you're my last regret,

I'm holding onto...

'cause you're the one I've been thinking lately,

Worthy enough to engulf the pain swiftly,

To bear the void your heart was pounding...

In fear,

That no one will get it,

But I did!

I know you're in need,

And so am I...

Feels so good to know

The one you need the most,

Needs you forever...

Holding you tight;

Shedding tears together,

Reminiscing the long-lost past

every night!

What we were made of

And what we are now...

I want to love us like,

My incomplete desires

Wires are interconnected in a way...

I never wanted to say,

But,

I've always loved you like I was never been shown before!

Howl

When night falls and the rest of the world is quiet...

I scream your name as loud as I can,

Thinking you might have heard me tonight!

But, somewhere I knew...

You were building broken houses,

Just like all these years...

You were pretending promises,

Oh! Your unpredictable shades,

One day, your lies would be so profound,

Unlike our everyday, your truth would feel so heavy!

Though I've seen, what belongs to you, eventually fades!

You would leave me feeling incomplete,

Saying your heart went cold!

Freeze like winter nights, bounded in a mould!

And still,

When night falls and the rest of my heart, starts decaying,

I dream your name as loud as I can,

Thinking you might have heard my silence, screaming!

A ray of hope

My years of unsaid feelings,

that I would scream in my poems...

You wore them,

Like there's an essence

You wanted me to smell...

How beautiful my scars are

When I carry them with grace!

Wait in that space

I wish I could stay

a little more,

Pretending for a while...

Hoping guilt,

realising that's delusional...

Weaving a tale in my mind,

Though I knew, you won't change!

But felt too enervated to resist,

Maybe a cursed senile!

Inquisition

And if the world was ending tonight!

Would you make my fears irrelevant?

Hugging me until I cry

Laughing through my bad days,

Would you have me in another life?

Or would you let me go,

Believing that there's no life beyond my grave…?

Grieving my death!

Flowering my memories every day.

Just a call away

Stabbed pain, bursting creatives...

Stammering every time I talk,

Still loud on papers!

Misleading emotions,

Efforts are never enough...

Losing interest every day,

I'm too tired to even ask for your love!

Sleeping unconscious...

Waiting,

I thought you were just a call away.

Holding me while I'm falling apart,

But you're shivering

I could see you,

Intentionally dancing the easy sway!

Frantic

Before I let you go,

I want to wait for the last time...

Don't know if it's apt,

as I think so,

This is a weird phase!

You changed like I am!

But that didn't fail me,

the way I feel,

unlike you...

More of a film!

Every day, I wake up staring at my phone...

Thinking, you would remember me now!

It feels so alone...

Sometimes, I pretend that you're here

talking to me, while I sleep.

But I know you ain't there.

And I can't,

I just can't sleep without listening to your voice...

I don't know why,

Maybe, I was the wrong choice!

Every time you hang up,

It breaks my heart!

But then I stare again...

Crying,

I still have your shirt.

I've got a feeling when this will end one day,

I will be lost,

There would be no coming back

No hands to pull me up

No one to hug me tight until I cry!

Hoping you would come, running back to me...

Though you'll be a stranger again!

But I'll try...

You've enough time,

I'm still waiting!

A night in your name love,

Just a call away!

It's my way of ensuring

that you remember me,

I'm not fading away!

I reconsider,

that I might be the last person you want

But at least make me feel

That I've got a place in your heart!

Or an infatuation...

To forget someone you loved.

I've broken my rules,

a million times!

No matter, how harsh you were

I went back to you

And you can't even try!

For once,

I promise it would be enough...

To be with you, all my life!

And if you don't,

I'll stop trying

Though my heart screams

saying, "No I won't!"

But I've to,

Learn to be happy without you!

To let you go,

If you want to be on the shore,

Waiting to touch my core,

Leaving me alone,

When it's done,

What you were looking for!

But that's how you are,

I know!

It's my fault,

That I loved a little more...

I was craving love,

Never felt it before.

The way you smile,

and the way you talk...

When you look at me

Though I never said...

'cause I was shy

But it felt alright!

Or even more, sometimes...

Like butterflies in my stomach

And a dreamy night...

I won't be able to stop

Thinking,

I would make more of you

In my mind!

But now, when I know...

I'm fading away

Slowly,

And you would forget me one day

I've decided to be happy by myself

Rubbing my scars gently...

Trying to heal,

A part of me, that was yours!

Though it's hard,

My gallery still fills you up

Your memories are in my heart!

Before I set you free...

I want you again!

So, we can undo the time,

And things we've done!

Though, I'll search for you,

When I'll see the stars

For you,

I'll be the moon...

Beautiful but full of scars!

I'll meet you again,

In another life...

To make sure you stay!

Until I die...

So, you can feel the pain

Screaming my name,

When it rains...

While staring at the sky!

Tears of pain

Every time I look at you,

It feels like a winding stream scared to

meet the boundless ocean,

Myriad of drowning skulls,

Dancing ballerinas...

A melody of their pain!

Whispering fears,

She wished to wail...

You looked so pale

Beneath the skin.

But you're trying to hold back;

Unknown suffocations of your mind

Lingering death of your beliefs,

Never letting you shine!

From frozen stillness to agonizing peers

in the blink of an eye!

When I look at you my love,

I wish you knew,

You're feeding darkness to your soul.

A strangulated world, we behold!

Imprisoned in my arms,

You clenched your fist,

Struggling,

But you won't let go!

Oh, so you know!

Just behind your closed doors,

There's sunshine,

You've missed all day long...

A deep blue sky,

Like oceans galore!

I want you to come back home,

I've been waiting,

While resting my head on your ghost heart

Tell me where have you been?

Fighting those winding streams,

Or,

Are you hiding again,

Pretending to be alive?

I know you're daydreaming!

I'm all ears, tell me about it...

"Don't leave me, humming your chosen tunes!"

The dreary bid of trying to sleep.

In a trice, the midnight touch of your palm on my skin

I could see the vehemence

In your nuances!

Emanated agony,

I could see tears streaming down your face;

Slowly caressed your forehead

With time, effaced by the rain!

Surrender

Leaving you was like,

A yard full of thorns...

Dying of thirst

amid an uninhabited desert,

Of sand storms!

Leaving you was like,

Her yearnings suffocating in disguise...

That, downpours might alleviate,

An oasis of calm;

Missing serenity...

She sighs!

4. Extremity

"To what is left beyond this earthly life, if death is the way, I may surrender my soul, forgetting love and whoever was holding me back, burying all my sins, forbidden longings!"

- *Chapter 34- Halt.*
- *Chapter 35- Hush*

Halt

Walking alone every day

had me thinking

If I got stuck in motion

entrapping my yearnings

letting time travel,

Then my hand starts twitching,

Seeing the clock startle

an offbeat rhythm,

While holding my grief,

my sorrows

till tomorrow.

Thus expelling my demons;

Cleansing my higher spirits,

Remembering Ouma,

and her green chilies knitted with lemons!

Her beliefs, my denial...

If your mind is hollowed

Reminiscing those fallen angels

living in your house!

A scar so shallow

That no one can save you from yourself

Neither would you,

An eminence of secret whereabouts!

Though I savored my endmost seclusion

Until there was no time to count on

Just so I could know,

The child in me while chasing those spring blooms

has touched innumerable autumn leaves,

Unfamiliar yet destructive

evolving stronger

deeper into the ocean of darkness

glowing like bioluminescent creatures

Beautifying their evil self,

gravitating light,

hypnotized to drown a life

To taste what the fear of death is like!

An intolerable pain

Conspired to trap a mind

Never letting it shine.

Bewildering truths, so believing safe lies...

Mirrors scathing reflections;

Bleeding mind, hideous blemishes on alluring faces

Inscrutable eyes begging everywhere.

Spinning them in circles

thus leaving them nowhere...

So what would it be like

to stop in time

Until the eruptions in my mind

Engulfing inflamed chaos in a mould

to pause them for a while!

An eerie glow of frozen and

unprecedented grey woods of my soul,

Sprinkled sinisterness into the ether of

erroneous and repellent sole,

Moving among infinite fermions…

Conversations of mind-numbing dinoflagellates

glowing fireflies everywhere,

devoted to boundless deliverance;

Quietuses, a fear of evanescence!

An imagination so fierce

suffocating truths hindered the passage of my tears.

A life led in ignorance,

The day has finally arrived!

Time couldn't bound me

But my grace,

An irrelevant fear of nothing but life

has drowned me to death!

While lying still,

My dreams held high

I could see someone staring

Beneath my skin

Flickering daydreams

And familiar sighs.

I could see,

glowing rage in her eyes...

Revenge she owned

Of bloodshed and pain

That I thought would go away one day!

But kept on penetrating,

A galaxy of frozen orbs sustaining no life.

Couldn't she fathom, that I professed to stay?

Not one word would she avow alife!

Entwined in each other's hearts,

Selfsame pulsating;

She was fearless...

To rip through my heaviness

Fettered cage,

gasping a sense of foreboding;

'cause I was floating,

A colossal of stellar hollowness!

Effaced memories,

Adored confidant,

Shoved my grave

Endured flash of remembrance

All my sins,

In the eyes of my beholder...

She wrecked my soul,

Wielding her dyrnwyn

Into the withered coldness;

An abated nuisance,

Began to ease

Oh, sol deep within the Ocean of Mercy!

Hush

Silence feels haunting

When the nights are pale,

Spent in miseries...

Reflections of the city lights and vehicles...

Raging and running,

leaving behind all the stories

they hold so close...

Photographs they carry,

flies away as the wind blows!

Teary eyes tired of searching for love

Compromises it all with the cigarette smoke,

She keeps looking through the window sill

The narrow streets lie alone,

Glowing lights and his memories...

She screams in fright!

Somehow at midnight,

3 a.m. shows how beautiful darkness can be!

The starlight she trapped in her lanterns never made her feel so free...

Earbuds and a little notepad she writes her poems on,

The saddest part of each song,

Oh, how it brings an ocean of unsaid words!

But today, everything seems unfair...

She struggles to sing the easiest lines,

There's silence yet again

And a blank page drowned in her tears,

Now, she is scared to even sleep with the lights on...

She prays to some unknown entity

where she's heard sometimes,

Aware that she was born within blazing stars,

A paradise adorned with emptiness...

Her existence is a nightmare

She's alive in her beliefs and daydreams!

But, she doesn't wish to exist as soon as the alarm rings...

Hush...

She is sleeping after a year full of rainstorms,

"wake up little girl!"

"I know you're tired of escaping all the ceaseless norms..."

Eyes filled with hopelessness and no tears left to cry,

Awake and sad...

Bleeding chapped lips,

Hands went through her tousled hair,

As she had endeavored to decipher

the frosty coffee lying inert beside her berth!

The warmth was gone,

She treasured love akin to a flightless bird,

To set her free, and let herself meld beneath the earth!

What have you seen?

From what she has shown,

She might be a pleaser to you...

A menial you've borrowed in your need,

But she is life's boundless ocean

where a feral brute quenches his thirst...

There's naught she can acquire from your rillet,

Neither she covets to!

For she is a bairn pertaining to silence...

Her heart was burning, fenced in amber!

She never feared forfeiting her chattels,

Though she was given insolence all of her life!

She withheld her grievances at the dead of each night,

Got rid of it all in her undressed poesy,

Engrossed in the tunes of a melancholic clavier...

Hush!

Her oscitant eyes seem to have sought solace in her chaotic silence...

So let her feel that stillness in her sleep;

Like myrtle in the meadows withered in the wake of her fragrance!

Until Next Time

Letting go of someone who's not meant for us is extremely important. That "someone" can be your inner demons as well. Oftentimes, it feels difficult to figure a way out but we should be aware of the fact that these feelings of fear, and isolation are temporary.

I solely believe that no matter how cruel life seems to be, the sun will rise again, and the demon hiding inside your soul will ultimately perish leaving all the darkness behind.

All these poetries are extremely personal and it took a lot of courage to exhale the emotions I had confined inside my heart. Midnight miseries and my hopeless desires continue to haunt me even now. But somewhere I believe, I shall be a happy poetess soon overcoming my weaknesses and creating a beautiful mess out of myself.

I shall always try to ignite my hope and write my heart out, something exceptional beyond the vulnerable emotions I've tangled my soul into.

Until Next Time...